mini
MYSTERIES

34
Tricky Tales
to Untangle

by Rick Walton
illustrated by Genevieve Kote

★ American Girl®

Published by American Girl Publishing
Copyright © 2004, 2006, 2007, 2015 American Girl

Questions or comments? Call 1-800-845-0005,
visit **americangirl.com**, or write to Customer Service,
American Girl, 8400 Fairway Place, Middleton, WI 53562-0497.

Printed in China
15 16 17 18 19 20 21 LEO 10 9 8 7 6 5 4 3 2 1

Editorial Development: Teri Robida, Judith Lary, Trula Magruder
Art Direction & Design: Sarah Boecher
Production: Jeannette Bailey, Judith Lary, Paula Moon, Kristi Tabrizi
Illustrations: Genevieve Kote

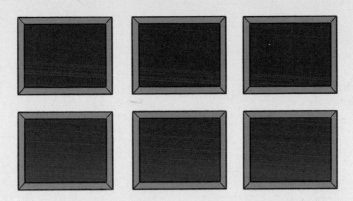

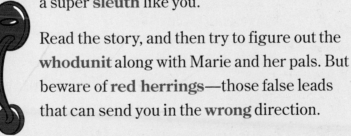

Dear Reader,

Do you like to crack **cases?** Uncover **clues?** Identify **suspects?** Look inside! You'll find a collection of mini **mysteries** waiting for a super **sleuth** like you.

Read the story, and then try to figure out the **whodunit** along with Marie and her pals. But beware of **red herrings**—those false leads that can send you in the **wrong** direction.

Once you think you've found a solution, open the detective's **door** inside the front and back covers of the book to check your answer.

Happy sleuthing!

Your friends at American Girl

Marie

Noelle

Sage

Rose

Contents

Brooke

Hailey

Hope

Faith

The Governor Is Calling

Someone's making prank calls—and Marie knows who!
What should she do now?

"May I speak with Marie Cantu?" the voice on the phone asked.

"This is Marie," answered Marie.

"Please hold for the governor."

Marie looked at the phone. Why would the governor be calling her? Marie waited for the governor to speak. She did help out at the animal shelter every weekend. And then there were her honors in English. Had she saved anyone's life lately?

She thought about these things as she waited . . . and waited . . . and waited. Finally, she realized the truth. Someone had played a trick on her!

She hung up the phone.

It rang again. Marie answered it. "Ha-ha-ha! Very funny," she said into the phone.

"Marie?" It was Noelle Dee, Marie's best friend and next-door neighbor. "I've been trying to call you for fifteen minutes, but your line was busy."

"Oh hi, Noelle. I just got a prank call. I thought it was the same person trying to call me again."

"The governor?"

"The governor," said Marie. "She called you, too? I waited for fifteen minutes before hanging up."

"I waited twenty minutes. Beat you," said Noelle. "Who do you think it was?"

"She disguised her voice, but now that I think about it, it sounded like Megan."

"I think we need to plan a little revenge. I'll be right over."

The girls discussed options, then headed over to Megan Brown's house.

It had been snowing all morning, and when Marie and Noelle reached Megan's, a blanket of snow covered the lawn, the sidewalk, everything. The girls walked up the sidewalk, making footprints in the spotless snow.

Marie whispered to Noelle. Noelle nodded. Then they went to work. Quietly they rolled snow into large balls. Together they pushed and heaved the balls up onto Megan's porch and built a large snowman, right in front of the door.

Then they rang the doorbell and ran to hide behind the neighbor's bushes.

Megan opened the door. "What's this?" she asked. She tried to push the screen door open. It moved just a few inches, but then it hit the snowman and would go no farther.

A few minutes later Megan emerged from behind the house. She stomped onto the porch and began to dismantle the snowman.

"Hi, Megan!" said Noelle. She and Marie walked up Megan's sidewalk as though they had just arrived. "Why are you building a snowman on your porch? Aren't you afraid it will block your door?"

"Very funny," said Megan. "I owe you one."

"No, we're even," said Marie. "So, how's the governor?"

"The governor? I don't know what you're talking about."

Marie told her about the prank calls.

"You think I made them?" asked Megan. "I wish. But I didn't. I walked over to the library this morning to work on my research report on Peru. I just got back ten minutes ago. Help me get this snowman off the porch, and we can go inside and get some hot cocoa."

Marie and Noelle helped Megan roll the rest of the snowman away from the door. Then the girls went in, sipped hot cocoa, and talked.

After a while, Marie stood up. "I'd better get going," she said. Noelle stood, too.

The girls started to leave. Then Marie turned back and said, "So tell me, Megan, who else did you call? Just us?"

"I told you, I didn't call you," said Megan.

"Oh, I think you did," said Marie. "You didn't go to the library today. I think you were here all morning being the governor's secretary."

How did Marie know that Megan hadn't gone to the library? The answer is calling you from behind door number 17.

Light Housekeeping

A dragon banister and a creaking door—have Marie
and Noelle's moneymaking plans gone too far?

"We're going to Hawaii! We're going to Hawaii!" Marie told Noelle,
a huge smile on her face.

"What a lucky family! I wish I could go," said Noelle.

"No," Marie said. "The 'we' is you and me! *We* are going to Hawaii.
My aunt Kristine has offered to take us with her to Hawaii!"

Noelle stared in shock at Marie for a second and then screamed,
"No way!"

"But there's a catch," Marie said. "Aunt Kristine wants us to earn
half the cost of our expenses. She'll pay the rest."

"How much will we need to earn?" Noelle asked. After Marie told
her, Noelle whistled. "That's a lot of
money. Do you think we can do it?"

"I think so," said Marie. "I've
already brainstormed ideas with my
parents. They know people who will
hire us for small jobs—starting with
Mrs. Peterson, the caretaker of that
huge historic house on Maple Street
that's open for tours."

The next day, Noelle and Marie went to Maple Street. Mrs. Peterson agreed to hire them to help clean the mansion before the tours began. The instant the friends stepped into the foyer of the elegant home, they realized what a big job cleaning it would be.

"Welcome, girls!" hailed Mrs. Peterson as she tap-tap-tapped across the glossy floor. "While I'm checking for cleaning materials, I've asked Gwen to show you around. She's training to be a tour guide and would like the practice."

"Hi! I'm Gwen," the older teen said. She stepped forward and changed to her tour-guide voice: "Let's start in the Great Hall, shall we?"

Gwen opened a door and flipped a switch. Electric lightbulbs on the chandelier lit up a thousand teardrop-shaped crystals, filling the room with light. Large chairs, sofas, ornamental tables, and statues furnished every corner.

"The owners held town meetings, dances, and banquets in this room. People loved the parties here."

"I'd have a party every night," Noelle said to Marie as she ran her hand along a fireplace mantel. She held up her fingers. "Not much dust. This should be easy."

"If we were just dusting *this* room," said Marie. "But cleaning this whole place will take forever."

Gwen pointed to the staircase. "Artisans hand-carved this banister. Notice the glass eyes of the dragons. Aren't they beautiful?"

"Beautiful and creepy," Marie whispered to Noelle.

Gwen led the girls through the house. "And here we have the dining room," Gwen said. "The family shipped the table from Italy and the grandfather clock from France."

Gwen flipped a switch next to a cabinet, and suddenly green-and-white china sparkled on the shelves. "Even the family's children knew to be careful with these treasures."

"I hope we don't break anything, either. That would cut into our savings for Hawaii," Noelle said.

"Good point," Marie replied. "Maybe we should just clean things that can't be knocked over or moved."

"That leaves the floor," joked Noelle.

"Imagine yourself gliding into this room for your first party," said Gwen, recalling a line in a script she had obviously worked hard to memorize. "You see this house—this room—*exactly* as it was two hundred years ago."

While the three girls imagined themselves in the past, the only sound they could hear was a ticking clock.

"We need to go," said Gwen quickly.

"Why?" asked Marie.

"I need to show you something I've never shown to anyone before today."

"Where's Mrs. Peterson?" asked Noelle. "Shouldn't we get to work?"

"This is more important." Gwen led the girls from room to room until they arrived at a door. "You won't believe this!"

Slowly Gwen turned the doorknob. She cracked open the door, slid her hand inside, flipped a switch, and screamed.

"Ah!" yelled Noelle and Marie as bright light poured over shelves stocked with cleaning supplies. All three laughed.

"Did you enjoy the tour?" Mrs. Peterson asked. She stepped from a small office into the room with the girls.

"Loved it!" Noelle exclaimed.

"And Gwen's a great tour guide," said Marie. "She excites you about the house. But she did have one small error in her tour script." Marie smiled at the teen.

"She did?" asked Mrs. Peterson.

"I did?" Gwen looked confused. And then she smiled. "Oh, yeah! Good catch. I noticed that on my first day and forgot to change it."

Exactly what did Marie catch?
To cast a little light on the subject, look behind door number 6.

The Neighbor's Garden

The girls volunteer for community service. Will they discover a hidden truth about a neighbor?

"I don't like the look of this place," said Sage Matthews.

Noelle shrugged. "It's just a little messy," she said.

"That's why we're here," said Hailey Ferris. "To help Mrs. Duncan clean up her yard."

"Messy?" said Sage. "Look at that garden. Who knows what's hiding under all those weeds."

"We're going to find out," said Marie.

Sage turned to Hailey. "When your mom asked us to help out your elderly neighbor, I was willing, but this place is really creepy."

The girls had arrived at Hailey's this Saturday morning dressed in work clothes and carrying hoes and rakes.

"Mom says Mrs. Duncan just can't get around like she used to," said Hailey. "She tinkers in her yard quite a bit, but she doesn't have

the energy to control her weeds. She'll really appreciate everyone's help."

"Well, hello, girls!" said Mrs. Duncan when she met them at her door. "Thank you so much for helping me. These old bones just don't move as well as I'd like them to."

"We're happy to help, Mrs. Duncan," said Hailey. "Where would you like us to start?"

"Oh, I don't know. There's so much to do. Anyplace you want to work is fine with me. I doubt you can get everything done that needs to be done, but anything you do will be a big help. I'm just happy to have you here."

"Why don't we each just choose a section of the yard and work on it?" said Marie. "I'll take the lawn. Mrs. Duncan, if you'll show me your mower, I'll make this lawn look beautiful."

"And I can trim your bushes," said Noelle.

"And I'll start weeding in your garden," said Hailey. "Sage, how about helping me?"

Mrs. Duncan was happy with the arrangement, and the girls set off to work.

"They all look like weeds to me," Sage confessed when she saw the garden.

"I'll show you which is which," said Hailey. "See these, with the long leaves that look like grass? Pull those out. And the ones with the thorns—pull those out, too. That's why we brought these gloves."

Hailey and Sage began weeding. Soon they heard the sound of clippers snapping at branches and the roar of the lawn mower.

And then a scream pierced the air.

Noelle dropped the clippers. Marie turned off the mower. They both ran to the garden.

There stood Sage, with a look of horror. She pointed at a mound of dirt. At the head of the mound was a stake. On a plaque on the stake was written "Angelica."

Then she pointed at another mound, another plaque, and the name "Rosemary."

Finally, the girls understood the scream. They all turned to look at a plaque at the head of a partially filled hole in the ground. On it was the name "Sage."

"What does this mean?" asked Noelle. "What do you know about Mrs. Duncan, Hailey?"

"I don't know," said Hailey. "She always seemed like a nice lady."

"I'm sure she is a nice lady," said Marie. "This is not what you think it is."

What did Marie know? To dig up the truth, open door number 7.

The Original Boston Brooke

No one expected to hear such an amazing story
from the new girl. But is it the truth or a big fat lie?

It was Saturday morning, and the first thing the people on Ivy
Street noticed when they went outside was the moving van parked at
the old Benson house.

Soon people began to gather. Some came to help carry in couches, tables, beds, an organ. Some came just to meet their new neighbors. But the kids arrived to see if there was anyone new their own age. For some of the girls, there was.

"My name's Marie," said Marie, and she stuck out her hand to the new girl. "This is Noelle and Hailey and Megan."

"Hi! I'm Brooke. Brooke Pinnock."

Suddenly questions started to fly.

"Where did you used to live?" asked Noelle.

"Boston."

"What grade are you in?"

"Fifth."

"What do your parents do?" Noelle had lots of questions.

"My parents aren't alive. I live with my grandparents. Grandpa just retired, and Grandma and Grandpa wanted to move to a smaller town. So here we are."

"Do you have any older brothers?" This was from Megan.

"Nope," said Brooke. "Do you?"

Megan shook her head no.

"What did your grandpa do before he retired?" asked Marie.

Brooke smiled. "He played for the Boston Red Sox."

Silence. And then Noelle asked, "Your grandpa played for a professional baseball team?"

"Sure," said Brooke. "He was good. The best. He also played for the Yankees, the White Sox, the Tigers, the Blue Jays—at one time or another, he played for every team in the American League. He played for forty years!"

"No one can play for that long," said Hailey.

"Grandpa did."

"That's impossible," insisted Megan. "He'd be worn out long before forty years were up."

"He did complain about arthritis in his fingers toward the end," said Brooke. "But besides that, he didn't seem to have much of a problem."

Megan stepped closer to Brooke. "Look, you don't have to lie to us—"

"I think she's just joking," said Hailey, giving the new girl a chance to change her story.

Brooke smiled and folded her arms. "Grandpa played for forty years. I'll bet anyone ten dollars that I'm telling the truth."

"I'll take that bet," said Megan.

"Hey, you don't *have* ten dollars—" started Noelle.

"—Me too!" interrupted Hailey.

"Wait a minute," said Marie as she watched the movers carry furniture inside the house. "I wouldn't take that bet if I were you. Brooke's telling the truth. Her grandfather did play for forty years, and he played for every American League team. Brooke just left out one important detail."

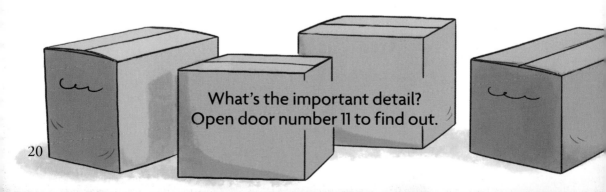

What's the important detail?
Open door number 11 to find out.

Shake, Rattle, and Roll Over

Marie and Noelle love pet-sitting, until a stray shows up.
Will the girls panic or put the dog in its place?

"Don't you love Ralphie?" Noelle asked. "He knows more tricks than we do!"

Mrs. Earl had hired Noelle and Marie to watch the Dalmatian while the Earls stayed at a lake cabin for the month. Every week Ralphie's trainer, Madeleine, stopped by to walk the dog to a nearby park for lessons. This week the girls tagged along.

Noelle and Marie watched as Madeleine ran Ralphie through his usual tricks: sit, stand, heel, shake, crawl, play dead, roll over, and speak.

"We have a new trick," said Madeleine. "Jump rope."

"Wow," Noelle whispered.

After Madeleine finished with the training, she invited Marie and Noelle to practice jumping with the dog. As the girls shouted out commands, an excited Ralphie showed his talents.

At the end of class, Madeleine hunched down next to Ralphie. She removed a blue metal charm from his collar and replaced it with a silver one. "You're moving up, Ralphie," she said, rubbing the dog's fur. "Before long, you'll wear gold!"

"Do you have a tight hold on his leash?" the trainer asked Marie.

"Sure," said Marie. "Why?"

Madeleine stood, smiled, and waved good-bye to Marie. Then, in a firm voice, she said, "Go home." Ralphie turned and raced toward his house, dragging a giggling Marie on the leash behind him.

Noelle dashed after them. "See you next week!"

Within minutes, the dog had slid onto the Earls' porch.

"Uh-oh, trouble," Noelle said, pointing to the garden.

A huge brown mutt sniffed and sifted through Mrs. Earl's tomato patch, ignoring the girls. "Think he'll fight with Ralphie?" asked Noelle.

"I doubt it," Marie said, "but we'd better be careful—"

Suddenly, before Marie could finish, Ralphie jerked the leash out of her hand and charged at the brown dog. The brown dog looked up, barked, and raced after Ralphie.

"Stop!" Marie shouted. "Ralphie, stop!"

But Ralphie didn't stop. He leaped at the other dog and put two front paws on the brown dog's side. Then the two dogs nipped at each other's necks. The dogs fell onto the lawn, wrestling and growling.

"Oh, no!" cried Noelle.

When the dogs heard Noelle, they stopped playing and turned to the girls, their tongues dangling in excitement.

"They're friends!" Noelle said.

"Who are you, big guy?" Marie asked.

"No name, but look!" Noelle pointed to a gold metal charm that dangled from the collar. "Madeleine's trained him."

"Hey, poochie. Where do you live?" Marie asked.

Ralphie jumped on top of the brown dog. After the girls laughed, he leaped on Noelle. "Down, Ralphie!" Noelle said. "Sit."

Ralphie sat. And so did the brown dog.

"See?" Noelle said. "Trained."

"Let me try something." Marie held out her hand to the brown dog and said firmly, "Shake."

The brown dog held out its paw. Ralphie held out his paw, too.

Marie stood up. "Roll over. Play dead. Speak." Both dogs obeyed each command.

"Madeleine *has* trained this dog," said Marie. "We could ask her where it lives, but we don't know where *she* lives."

"If Madeleine's trained this dog, then it knows her commands," said Noelle.

"And?"

"And we'll find out where it lives," Noelle said.

"How?"

"You'll see," said Noelle.

How did Noelle find out where the brown dog lived?
Peek behind door number 16 for the answer.

An Elephant for President?

Someone's trying to ruin Marie and Noelle's campaign. Could it be . . . the boys?

The campaign poster showed an elephant with a girl's head on it. A long trunk stretched out from the girl's head. The caption read, "Vote for Marie Cantu—she *nose* what to do."

Marie admitted it was a clever idea, but she really *was* planning to run for student body president, and this silly poster could hurt her chances.

"Cute," said Noelle. "I've never seen a brown-haired elephant."

"Let me show you something really bad." Noelle dragged Marie down the hall to another taped-up poster. This one had a hippopotamus with Noelle's head on it. Noelle's curly brown hair hung to the ground.

This campaign slogan said, "Hippo, Hippo, Hurray! Noelle Dee for Lincoln Middle School Vice President!"

"That is bad," Marie said. "They're all over the school. Everyone's seen them!"

"Who do you think did it?" asked Noelle.

"I have no idea, but it's someone who doesn't want us—"

"—elected." Noelle broke in, finishing Marie's sentence as she often did. The girls dropped their notebooks to take the posters down, but just then the bell rang. School was starting. The posters would have to wait.

At morning recess, Marie and Noelle grabbed three of their friends—Rose James, Sage Matthews, and Faith Peterson—to help take down posters. But as they walked up and down the halls, they found that the posters were already gone.

"Did you see them?" asked Marie.

"Everybody saw them," said Faith.

"Thank goodness the custodian took them down."

"Too bad," said Faith. "I wanted one as a souvenir. They were funny."

The girls talked as they walked out to the playground.

"They *were* funny," said Noelle, "but they might cost Marie and me the election. We want to find out who put them up."

"Probably one of the boys," said Sage.

"Possibly," added Marie. "But it looks like the poster maker knew we were planning to run, and we've told only a few friends."

"Couldn't have been me," said Sage. "I'm not a good enough artist to have made those posters. Rose, you're a great artist. You could have made the posters."

Rose flipped her dark brown hair defiantly. "I've been staying with my grandma all week, and all my art supplies are at home, so I couldn't have made the posters."

"What posters?" Hope Harrison asked as she walked up to the group.

"Where've you been?" asked Sage. "*The* posters. They were plastered all over the school. Of Marie and Noelle running for president and vice president."

"I just got back from the dentist. Haven't been to school yet. So, you have your posters up already?" asked Hope. "Cool! I've been thinking of running myself, but I'll just vote for you two instead. Then, when you win, you can make me Secretary of State or something."

"They're joke posters," said Rose. "Someone put Marie and

Noelle's heads on animals' pictures. We're trying to find out who made them."

Marie crossed her arms. "Maybe you *should* run, Hope. Everyone's seen these posters, and they might have ruined our chances at winning. So it might as well be you. Then, when you win, you can make me ambassador to France."

"Oh, you'll still win," said Hope.

Marie wasn't as confident as Hope was that she and Noelle would win. "Let's get back to the mystery," she said. "Who would have put up those posters?"

"Faith," said Rose, "you've been really quiet. Where were you this morning?"

"I was right behind you, walking to school. You saw me. And, no, I didn't make the posters."

Hope leaned over to Sage. "I wish I could have seen the posters. Were they really funny? Who was on the hippo?"

"Noelle was on the hippo," answered Sage. "Marie was on the elephant." And then Sage whispered, "And, yes, the posters were funny. I still think it was one of the boys."

"There's a lot we can blame them for," said Marie. "But not this." She smiled at Noelle. "I know who made the posters, and she's standing right here."

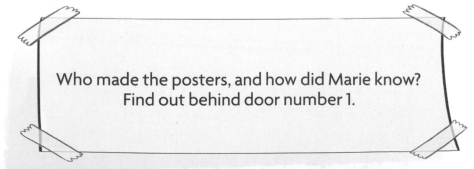

Who made the posters, and how did Marie know?
Find out behind door number 1.

Letters from an Admirer

Someone really likes Noelle. But is it the person she thinks it is?

"Did you get my cousin's letter?" Ben asked Noelle. "He said he was going to write you as soon as he got home."

"Did I ever," said Noelle. "So far he's sent five letters."

"What's this?" asked Marie. "You haven't told me this. Come on, spill it."

"It's nothing," said Noelle, blushing. "It's just . . . well . . . Ben introduced me to his cousin Joseph a little over a month ago when he was visiting. Joseph didn't talk to me much. But I keep getting letters from him. I just opened this one." She held up the letter.

"Let me read it," said Marie. She took the letter from Noelle's hand and read it to herself:

Dear Noelle,

Can't write much. Very busy. Just wanted to drop you a note from Williamsburg. You and my cousin Ben should come out sometime.

Well, gotta go. Tell my cousin I said "hi".

I miss you. You know how much I like you.

Joseph

P.S. Did you get the locket I sent you? I saw it in a shop yesterday and knew you would like it.

Marie looked at the envelope. The letter had been sent from Williamsburg two days ago. "I'd love to visit the east coast, too," said Marie.

"Joseph's been sending me a letter every week," Noelle said. "He's so thoughtful."

"Wow," said Marie. "He must really like you."

"I'm jealous," said Ben. "He hasn't sent me any letters—or called since he left. So, did you get the locket? What does it look like? Do you like it?"

"I do," said Noelle. "It has a raccoon on the front, and a photo of a raccoon inside. How did he know I like raccoons?"

"How would he not?" said Ben. "You're always drawing raccoons on your notebooks."

"Yeah, maybe," said Noelle. "And I must have been wearing my raccoon T-shirt when we met."

Marie had a funny look on her face. She said, "The guy who sent you that locket, and the letters, must really like you. Maybe someday he'll be brave enough to tell you."

"But he has," said Noelle. "Joseph tells me he likes me in every one of his letters."

"No, I don't think he does," said Marie.

What did Marie mean? For a letter-perfect answer, open door number 12.

Taken for a Ride

The girls love scary roller coasters, but could Sage's little brother be the bravest of them all?

"Am I tall enough for this ride?" asked Noelle. She stood next to the sign with the bear holding its paw at 48 inches, the minimum height for riders on all the scariest rides at Liberty Amusement Park.

"Not quite," joked Marie. "Maybe in ten or twenty years. You'd better stick with the baby boats."

Marie and her friends had volunteered to bring the younger Ivy Street kids to the park. Hailey chaperoned her younger sisters, Nicole and Emma. Sage had agreed to babysit her little brother, Joey. And Hope had asked to escort Caitlin, another of Hailey's sisters, around the park. Kenny, Noelle's little brother, preferred to wash the car with his dad, so Marie and Noelle were on their own.

They'd all arrived early and spread out through the park grounds, agreeing to meet at the Washington Pavilion at noon for lunch.

After a few hours of riding, Noelle and Marie climbed into The Flipper, strapped themselves in, and pulled down the bar. Over and over the girls tumbled as the ride went around and around, up and down. Now they were looking at the sky; now they were looking at the ground.

And when the ride stopped, and they finally tumbled off, Noelle said, "I think I . . . whoa!"

She caught hold of a lamppost to keep herself from falling. "I think I need to sit down."

"It's about noon," said Marie. "Let's go to the pavilion. It's so hot, and I could use a soda."

At the pavilion, Marie reached into the ice chest they'd brought. Everyone had been assigned to bring something for the picnic. Marie and Noelle had brought a dozen bottles of pop.

"Someone's beat us here," said Marie. She pointed to the ice chest.

Ten bottles of pop stood there in the ice. Two bottles were missing.

Marie and Noelle each pulled out a bottle, twisted off the cap, and began to drink. The cold pop was just what they needed to cool off and settle their still-tumbling stomachs.

"I'm hungry," said Caitlin, who walked up holding a stuffed cat. "When can we eat?"

"I think it's too hot to eat," added Hope. "I'm just thirsty."

"Is it time for lunch yet?" It was Sage, with Joey. The boy reached up to hold his sister's hand.

"Hey, Sage," said Noelle. "Been on a lot of the rides today?"

35

"Oh, yeah," said Sage. "This kid just won't stop. He made me take him on The Colossus four times." The Colossus was the park's giant roller coaster, with corkscrews and steep plunges—the park's most popular attraction.

"And he didn't lose his lunch?" asked Noelle.

"Lunch!" said Joey. "I want lunch."

"Soon, Joey," said Sage. "Yeah, Joey loves the scary rides. I'm the one who can hardly stand them!"

"Lunch!" shouted Joey.

"I think it's close enough to noon to eat," said Marie. "Why don't we break out some sodas and sandwiches, and while we're eating, Sage can tell us what she and Joey were really doing."

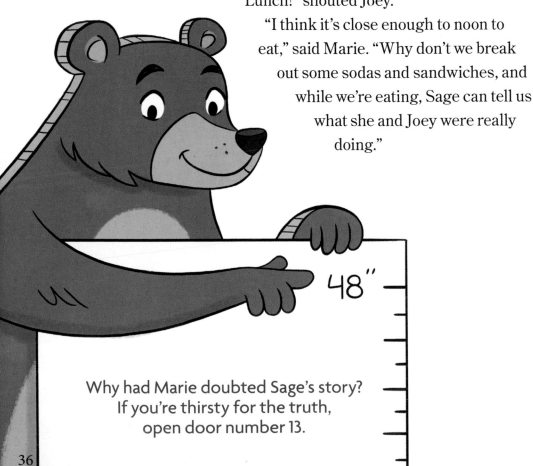

48"

Why had Marie doubted Sage's story?
If you're thirsty for the truth,
open door number 13.

Not Cool

It's a tie. Now Marie must choose between two plans.
Will her choice hurt three very close friends?

"We could hire skywriters," said Sage.

"If we were rich," said Rose. "But we can create a mascot, Billy the Bully. The police could arrest him."

"How would we bring police to our school?" asked Hailey.

The girls sat on Noelle's back porch drinking lemonade and brainstorming ideas for a citywide anti-bullying contest. The winner would earn a $525 cash reward and a certificate.

"Why don't we just change our school's name to 'Friendly Elementary?'" added Hailey.

"Oh, much easier to do," said Rose sarcastically. "I hope Marie arrives soon. She has good ideas. Where is she?"

"She's entertaining visiting cousins," Noelle said. "But she'll be here. Besides, we can develop ideas, too."

"Let's ship all the bullies to Antarctica," Brooke suggested. "They'll be so cold that they'll promise to be good."

"OK, so maybe we can't develop good ideas," said Noelle. The friends all laughed.

"Get serious," Noelle said. "We have a trip to Hawaii at stake."

"Maybe for you and Marie," said Hope. "But I plan to add to my savings for a new bike."

"School clothes for me," said Rose, raising her hand.

"A cute bedroom comforter," Sage chimed in. "Mine's still got ducks on it."

"I love ducks!" said Brooke. "In fact, I'm donating my cash to the animal shelter."

"I plan to surprise my mom with a special gift for her birthday," added Hailey. "It's coming up soon."

"We can't buy anything without a plan that will amaze the city," said Noelle.

"Let's do this!" urged Hailey.

The group agreed to focus on the contest instead of the reward. Brooke wrote every idea the team had into a notebook. After they had twenty ideas, Brooke read each one aloud. If the idea involved too much money or time, or too many people, the girls cut it. In the end, two ideas remained: a pencil promotion and a buddy plan. And then the team voted.

"Sorry I'm late," Marie said, bursting onto the back porch. "My cousins just left. Any progress?"

"The good news," Noelle said. "We have two ideas."

"Awesome!" Marie cheered. "And the bad news?"

"Three voted for plan one. Three voted for plan two. That leaves you to break the tie."

"Bummer," said Marie. "Well, let's hear them."

"Plan one we call 'Buddies, Not Bullies,'" Brooke said. "We team older kids with younger ones. Older kids read to younger ones, help with homework, and become their friends. Kids who have good friends don't usually bully others."

"Cool idea," said Marie. Noelle, Brooke, and Hope nodded enthusiastically. The three of them loved this idea.

"And the second?"

"We call plan two 'The Write Stuff,'" said Sage.

She handed Marie a pencil.

Marie took the pencil and examined it. Sage had written from point to eraser: TOO COOL TO BE MEAN.

"The city prints a pencil for each student. The students see the slogan in class every day, and it begins to sink in," said Sage.

Hailey, Rose, and Sage felt strongly that this plan would fit the school's budget *and* be a big success with students.

Marie held up the pencil. She put her thumb over the point, covering half the pencil. Then she shook her head and said, "We should go with the buddy idea."

"We three like the pencil plan," Hailey said. "You're just siding with Noelle. Let's enter both ideas and see who wins."

"I like the idea, but it won't work," said Marie.

"It will," said Rose, "and we'll have a better chance at winning if we enter both ideas."

"Yeah," said Sage. "If I have to stare at those ducks for much longer, I'll start quacking up."

The girls laughed at Sage.

"Just listen to me and then decide," said Marie. "I'm afraid the pencils will eventually send the wrong message."

What wrong message did Marie think the kids would get? Get to the point behind door number 4.

40

Sticks and Stones

What will the girls of Acorn Cabin do now?
One of their trail clues doesn't make sense!

"We know it's hot," said Erica, the head camp counselor, "so we have a treat to help you cool off." Marie and Noelle listened to Erica with anticipation. They had been at Camp Veronica Lake for three sweltering days.

Erica nodded to four other counselors, who were standing behind coolers on the far side of the campfire pit. The four, in unison, opened the cooler lids. "Popsicles!" they shouted.

Everyone cheered.

"Have all you want," Erica said. "But wrappers go in the trash, sticks in this bucket. We're going to use them later for a project." She pointed at a bucket near her feet. "And don't feed the squirrels," she added. The camp was full of the cute creatures, all begging for any hint of food. They were hard to resist.

At two o'clock, after a break, the girls gathered again at the campfire pit.

"We have something fun for you," said Erica. "A challenge. Each cabin has been assigned a different path through the woods."

As she spoke, she handed a folded piece of paper to one girl from each of the six cabins. "All paths lead to a secret location, where we'll have our next activity. Your cabin counselors have gone ahead and marked your trail. Last cabin group to the end gets dinner cleanup. The paper I gave you tells where your trail begins. Now, go!"

Marie and Noelle were in Acorn Cabin along with Christina, Sarah, and Annika. Christina unfolded the paper. "Behind the latrines." Eww!

The girls headed for the latrines. Behind them they found a trail. At the head of the trail was a star made out of purple-stained Popsicle sticks. "Someone loved grape," said Marie.

Noelle bent down closer to the star. "So that's why they saved the sticks."

The five girls headed down the trail. At the first fork in the path, a Popsicle-stick arrow pointed them to the right.

At the second fork, Popsicle sticks on the right trail spelled "NO." Sticks on the left trail spelled "YES." The girls headed left.

At the third fork, there was a large flat stone. On the stone, Popsicle sticks spelled out "L I F T."

"Lift?" asked Noelle. "We're supposed to lift the rock? It's huge! We can't lift it."

"Let's try," said Sarah. "There must be something under it that

tells us where to go next. If all five of us lift, maybe we can move it."

They tried. They failed. The rock wouldn't budge.

"A lever," said Annika, the tallest of the girls. "We're supposed to figure out how to lift the rock. We need to find a lever." The girls looked until they found a long, dead branch. Annika shoved an end under the rock, and the girls all pushed down on the branch.

Snap! The branch broke. The girls tumbled to the ground.

"Maybe we're supposed to lift just the sticks," said Sarah.

"And when we lift the sticks, what?" asked Annika. "The earth will open up, revealing a secret tunnel?"

"No," said Sarah. "But maybe there's something written under them." She lifted the sticks, one by one. Nothing.

"Let's pick a trail and take it," said Annika. "If we just stand here, we're guaranteed to get dinner cleanup. If we pick a trail, we have a fifty-fifty chance of choosing the right one."

"And a fifty-fifty chance of getting lost," said Noelle.

"Look!" said Christina. "I've found it!" She pointed to three sticks that were lying on the trail to the right. "This means we're supposed to take the right branch. Let's go."

Marie grabbed her. "Wait." She looked at the sticks on the trail. She looked at the sticks on the stone. "I know what the clue is. We're supposed to take the left branch!"

What is the clue that made Marie choose the left branch?
Stick with the answer behind door number 3.

Play with Your Feud

Just before opening night, the stars of the play refuse
to look at each other. Will the show ever go on?

The rehearsal for the spring play wasn't going well.

The scenery wasn't ready. Some of the actors didn't have all their lines memorized. Nerves were getting frayed.

And then things blew up.

"I will not work with Sage!" said Hope.

"And I won't talk to Hope!" added Sage.

This was quite a problem. Hope and Sage were the stars of the play *The Pet Shop,* which parents, teachers, and students would all turn out to see tomorrow night!

"That's just great," groaned Matt. He scratched at his hot, furry costume. "How can we rehearse? Girls—"

"—Girls, girls," interjected Mrs. Mahoney, the play's director. "Calm down. Let's be nice and get back to work. Oh, I hate it when you fight!"

Mrs. Mahoney had been the spring play's volunteer director ever since her first child had entered Lincoln Middle School thirty-five years ago. Even after her last child had graduated, she kept directing. She was a sweet lady, patient with the students and a good play director, but she was horrible at resolving conflicts.

"I refuse to rehearse if I have to look at Sage," said Hope.

"Fine with me," said Sage. "I hope I never have to see you again!" She swung around, and her long mouse tail followed.

"Girls, girls," said Mrs. Mahoney. "Please."

But Hope and Sage, cat and mouse, crossed their arms and glared—at each other.

"Come on, you're wasting our time," Matt said. "This costume is getting really hot!"

"Grow up, you two," said Megan, walking from behind a curtain to center stage. "I have a line and I want to get it over with! Rehearse with your eyes closed."

"I'd keep my eyes closed," said Sage, "but I don't trust Hope to keep hers closed, and I don't want her looking at me anymore!"

"Please, ladies," said Mrs. Mahoney, her arms filled with various headbands decorated to look like a bunny, a puppy, and a guinea pig. "You're actors. Pretend you like each other!"

Noelle could feel the tension on the stage, which resembled a giant pet shop. "Rehearse back-to-back!" she suggested.

"She would back into me just to crush my tail," said Sage.

"We'll blindfold you," said Megan.

"That would mess up my ears," replied Hope, adjusting the pointed yellow felt.

"Let's just replace them," sighed Matt, tugging at the zipper on the front of his spotted suit.

"Oh dear, we can't do that," said Mrs. Mahoney. "The play's tomorrow night, and they're the only ones who know their lines. Oh, what are we going to do?"

"Mrs. Mahoney?" Marie stepped up. "I know how Sage and Hope can face each other, keep their eyes open, and practice without looking at each other or touching each other."

"We can't turn off the lights," said Mrs. Mahoney. "That would be too dangerous."

"We won't turn off the lights," said Marie.

"Then go ahead," said Mrs. Mahoney. "Right now I'm willing to try almost anything."

Marie whispered something to Noelle, who nodded and then hurried backstage. "Sage? Hope? Close your eyes," said Marie.

"They're already closed," snapped Hope.

Marie took Sage and moved her up near the front of the stage. She turned Sage's back to the audience. "Don't back up," said Marie, "or you'll take an unhappy trip."

Marie then took Hope and moved her so that she was standing six feet in front of Sage, facing her.

"There!" Marie smiled. "Noelle, are you ready?"

"Ready!" Noelle answered.

"GO!" shouted Marie.

A few seconds later, Marie spoke to the girls. "Open your eyes and get back to rehearsing!"

What did Marie do so that Hope and Sage
could practice without looking at each other?
Play detective—then open door number 15.

Up, Up, and A-What?

Noelle discovers a message while floating in a hot-air balloon. But what does the message mean?

"You're going to love it," gushed Hailey. "It's not scary at all!"

"We'll see about that," said Marie, who was afraid of heights.

It was the day of the big balloon festival. Dozens of hot-air balloonists had come from all over the country to fly their balloons.

One of those balloonists was Carol Ferris, Hailey's mom. Mrs. Ferris had told Hailey she could invite a couple of friends to take a ride. Hailey had invited Marie and Noelle.

"Are you sure there's room for all of us?" asked Marie, sizing up the small basket. "If there's not, I could stay down here, and you all could go up."

"There's plenty of room," said Mrs. Ferris.

"How about your other girls?" Marie asked. "Don't they want to go riding with their mom?"

"My daughters have been up with me a thousand times."

"At least," Hailey added.

"Besides, they said they have a project to do this morning," said Mrs. Ferris.

"I think that project is watching cartoons in their pajamas," Hailey whispered to Marie and Noelle.

"So, climb in, girls," said Mrs. Ferris, "and we'll be off into the wild blue." Hailey stepped into the basket and then moved to the back to give Noelle and Marie room. Noelle climbed in, smiling. She loved to fly but had never done anything so adventurous as this! Marie hesitated outside the basket until Noelle reached out to help her in.

"She's just nervous," explained Noelle. To Marie she said, "Don't worry. I'll hold on to you."

"I was nervous the first time I went up in a balloon, too," said Mrs. Ferris. "But you get used to it. Besides, no one's ever fallen out of *my* basket."

"I wasn't nervous my first time," said Hailey.

"You were two years old your first time," replied Mrs. Ferris. "You didn't know any better."

Hailey's mom showed Marie and Noelle what to hold on to and explained how the balloon worked. Then slowly, gently, they began to rise.

"If you open your eyes, you'll enjoy it more," Noelle said to Marie. "This is incredible!"

Marie held on tightly to the basket and slowly opened her eyes. It *was* incredible. She peered down as the earth fell away below her and the cars, the people, everything grew smaller and smaller. She watched in awe as they passed over their school, over the grocery store where her parents shopped, over streets, houses, and fields.

"Look," said Noelle, pointing down at the field over which they were flying. "I see a bunch of letters."

Below them someone had formed, with sheets and blankets, five huge letters: W O W I H.

"Someone's excited," said Hailey.

"Yeah," said Mrs. Ferris. "I wonder what it means."

"It's a message, Mrs. Ferris," said Marie. "And it's for you."

How does Marie know the message is
for Mrs. Ferris, and what does it mean?
Look behind door number 10 for the answer.

BOO!

Hailey discovers a message from a ghost. Should she decode its meaning, reply, or just go back to sleep?

You're not supposed to go to sleep early at a sleepover.

And you're not supposed to go to sleep at all after watching a scary movie.

But the girls had chased each other all day in sprinkler tag, water balloon fights, and sponge tag. After a dinner of pizza and ice cream sundaes, somewhere about the time the ghost first appeared in the movie, the girls dropped off to sleep.

So by the time the haunted movie family found out who the ghost really was, all the girls were out. They lay, like mummies in a tomb, wrapped in their blankets on Brooke's bedroom floor.

And then suddenly—a scream!

The lights flipped on.

Marie, who had fallen asleep in a chair, looked around, confused. The first thing she saw was herself, reflected in the window. The second thing she saw was the clock on the nightstand showing 10:08. Just then it clicked over to 10:09. They had all been asleep for about an hour. Marie turned to see who had screamed.

Noelle stood at the light switch. "It was Hailey who screamed!" shouted Noelle. "Look!"

Hailey looked scared. Her eyes were wide and she was shivering.

"What's wrong, Hailey?" asked Brooke. "Did you have a nightmare?"

"N-n-n-no," said Hailey. "Well, yeah, I did. I was dreaming about ghosts haunting a family. Like in the movie. But then I woke up. And I saw the word 'BOO!'"

"Are you sure it wasn't just part of the dream?" asked Noelle. "You can wake up and still be dreaming."

"I was awake," said Hailey. "But I wasn't dreaming. I'm sure of it. I saw the word 'BOO!' right over there somewhere."

Hailey pointed at one of the walls. Marie followed Hailey's finger to a nightstand with a few books, a lamp, and a digital clock. She also saw a window with open curtains and a painting of a cat.

"I'll bet it was that cat picture," said Noelle. "Look at those big eyes, like two big Os, as in 'BOO.' And cats' eyes glow in the dark."

"It wasn't the cat picture," said Hailey. "I saw the word 'BOO!' Besides, that's a painting of a cat. Painted eyes don't glow in the dark."

"They do if you use glow-in-the-dark paint," said Noelle. "It's the latest."

"My cat's eyes have never glowed before," said Brooke, who sounded scared. "So I believe Hailey!"

"Then check the window," said Noelle. "Maybe someone was playing a joke."

"The window's closed," said Brooke. "And locked."

"Maybe someone held something in the window," said Noelle. "You know those neighbor boys!"

"If it's a ghost," Brooke said, trying to act calmer, "I think we'd all better sleep in another room."

"Or another house," added Hailey.

"Or maybe we should all just go back to sleep here," said Marie. "There were no neighbor boys. And there was no ghost. And Hailey was awake. And she did see something. But it wasn't 'BOO!'"

What had Hailey seen? The answer's on the other side of door number 14.

My Summer Vacation

Vacation memories turn into a mystery when the teacher decides to tell her tale.

There are several important things that you're required to do the first day back at school after summer vacation.

You have to find out if you're lucky enough to have some of your friends in your classes (and if you get to sit by them). You have to see if your homeroom teacher is going to be strict or nice. And you have to hear about what everyone did over the summer.

Marie and Noelle met the first requirements. They were in many of the same classes, and their homeroom teacher said they could sit together as long as they didn't disrupt class. They'd convinced her that they should sit together because they were the new student body president and vice president, and they had to plan.

Brooke and Hailey were also in their class.

Their homeroom teacher, Ms. Toone, seemed very nice (though the girls had learned from past years that a class that goofed off too much could make a nice teacher quite cross).

That left summer vacation.

All the kids had had a chance to say what they'd done during the summer. Marie and Noelle told about their beach vacation, about

summer camp, and about their first balloon rides.

Hailey told about the trip she'd taken with her father to Brazil.

Brooke described her travels to Boston with her grandfather, who was honored for having played the organ at baseball games for so many years. The Red Sox team all signed a ball for Brooke's grandfather, who then gave the ball to Brooke.

After the students described their adventures in detail, Ms. Toone spoke up.

"I did something very exciting this summer, too," said the teacher. "But I'm going to give you some clues and you're going to have to figure out what it was."

Marie and Noelle leaned forward. They loved a challenge.

Ms. Toone continued. "I saw four states in a couple of seconds."

"What did she say?" Marie asked.

"I'm not sure," replied Noelle.

Ms. Toone went on. "I didn't drive through or fly to all four states, though."

"No one can walk that fast!" said Matt. "And time machines haven't been built yet."

"But the most fun I had," she continued, "is when I pulled out the game Twister and played in all four states at the same time. Anyone want to guess where I went?"

Marie reached into her desk and pulled out a pocket atlas. She pointed at something on the page for Noelle. Then Marie's and Noelle's hands shot up.

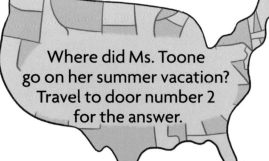

Where did Ms. Toone go on her summer vacation? Travel to door number 2 for the answer.

The Slogan Showdown

A slogan contest incites a battle of wills.
Who will be a winner, and who will be revealed?

"I don't know about you, but my brain's fried," Noelle said.
She sat on a low branch of an oak tree in her backyard. Marie, Brooke,
and Hailey lay on the lawn below.

"It's a $500 first prize!" Brooke said. "Think of something."

"We've thought of a hundred ideas," Hailey said. "None of them are
any good."

After winning the city's anti-bullying contest, the girls had entered
every contest they could find. They hadn't won anything else, but they
felt confident that eventually the perfect contest would turn up.

The perfect contest turned out to be one to create a new slogan for
their town. Liberty hoped to attract new businesses and more
tourists—and needed a good slogan.

"Let's take a break," Marie said. "Or at least find a change of location to inspire us."

"I know a great place!" Noelle jumped down out of the tree. "Our
kitchen. Let's brainstorm and eat lunch."

The girls headed for Noelle's house. *SLAM!* went the back screen
door as they entered the utility room that led to the kitchen.

"Sorry. Dad needs to fix that door spring," said Noelle.

"Sandwiches?" she asked. Noelle took bread from a bread drawer and set it on the table. Then she leaned into the fridge and passed food to outstretched hands: roast beef, sliced turkey, mayonnaise, and mustard.

The girls created their sandwiches in silence.

Then Brooke offered, "How about, 'Give Me Liberty or Give Me Death!'"

"George Washington said that," said Nicholas, Noelle's brother, who walked into the kitchen from the living room with his friend Colton.

"Actually, Patrick Henry said that," said Hailey. "It would make a gruesome slogan."

"Are you entering the slogan contest?" Nicholas asked. "We are, too! And as soon as we figure ours out, we're racing to the mayor's office and entering it. If two people come up with the same slogan,

and it wins, the first one who entered it gets the prize."

"So, what's your slogan?" asked Colton.

"Like we'd tell you," said Noelle. "You'll race to the mayor's office and enter it as your own."

"Don't worry," said Nicholas. "We're leaving. Come on, Colt." The two boys left through the utility room.

"Back to brainstorming," said Noelle. The room fell silent again as the girls kept thinking.

"Wait a minute," Brooke suddenly shouted. "I have an amazing idea! It's utterly perfect. How about—"

"How about we wait a second," Marie interrupted. She tiptoed to the utility-room door and yanked it open. Nicholas and Colton fell forward and crashed to the floor.

"Eavesdroppers," Hailey said.

"Nick!" Noelle shouted. "Out!"

"OK, OK," said Nicholas.

After the boys left, Hailey asked, "How did you know they had hung around, Marie?"

How did Marie know? Open door number 13 to find out.

Poor Little Puppy

Fluffball is missing! But who could have taken the dog right out from under the girls' noses?

"Fluffball's so cute!" said Sage, showing a photograph to her friends as they walked home from school.

"Oh, I want to see her," whined Hope. "I love puppies."

"Me, too," said Noelle. "What will you do if someone claims her?"

"It's been a month since we found her," said Sage. "Animal Control says she's ours now. They think someone just abandoned her."

"Poor thing!" said Noelle.

"How could anyone abandon a puppy like that?" asked Marie. "She's adorable!"

"I don't know," said Sage. "She must have been so frightened, all alone in the streets."

"When can we see her again?" asked Hope.

"How about tonight?" Sage answered. "I'll ask Mom if we can have a sleepover. Let's start at 6:30."

At 6:30, Sage opened the door for her friends. "You got here just in time," she said. "We're about to have a storm."

As though on cue, the thunder cracked. Immediately, from behind Sage, came a loud, sharp barking. The barking continued ferociously as Sage moved aside, revealing a poodle puppy.

"She always barks at thunder," shouted Sage over the roar.

Finally the racket stopped. "I don't know what's louder: the thunder or the dog," said Marie.

"She *is* loud," said Sage. "Poor thing. I hope she gets over it."

Hope reached down to pick up Fluffball, but the puppy scurried away and hid behind Sage's legs.

"She's a very clingy dog," said Sage. "She follows me everywhere. But once she gets used to you, I think she'll let you pet her."

The girls admired Fluffball. Then Sage said, "Let's get something to eat."

"Sounds good to me," said Hope.

The girls headed to the kitchen with Fluffball close at Sage's heels.

"How about grilled cheese?" asked Sage's mom when the girls told her they were hungry.

"I love grilled-cheese sandwiches," said Marie.

Sage's mom pulled out a frying pan, bread, butter, and cheese, and the girls offered to help. Fluffball begged at their feet until Sage gave her a bite of cheese. The puppy gobbled down the cheese and then sniffed around the kitchen for more.

"At least she's not hanging around your feet," said Marie.

"Yeah," said Sage. "That's a good sign. Maybe she's feeling more comfortable. She likes to explore, but she always stays in the same room with me."

Sage's mom flipped the sandwich in the pan. The toasted side was a perfect golden brown.

"Almost ready," said Sage. "The only thing we need now is root beer. There's some in the garage. I'll go out and get it."

By the time Sage returned with the soda, Sage's mom had the sandwiches on the table. "Smells good," said Sage.

The sandwich platter was almost empty when thunder clapped again. The girls covered their ears, expecting to hear Fluffball's barking.

But all they heard was silence.

They looked around. "Where's Fluffball?" asked Noelle. "I don't hear her."

Sage jumped up and poked around the kitchen. With the other girls' help, she searched under chairs and in drawers and cabinets. She even opened the refrigerator.

No Fluffball.

"I'm worried," said Sage. "Where is she?"

"Let's spread out and look for her," said Marie.

The girls crawled under beds, peeked behind sofas and chairs, ducked under tables, and poked in closets. They searched every room in the house.

No Fluffball.

"She's gotten out and run away!" said Hope.

"Oh, no!" said Sage. "In this storm? She'll be scared . . . and soaked."

"Let's think about this," said Noelle. "When was the last time we saw Fluffball?"

After a moment. Marie smiled. "I think I know where she is!"

And Marie led the girls right to Fluffball.

Where was the frightened little puppy? Search behind door number 16 for the answer.

66

The Long, Dark Hall

Someone's following Marie and Noelle down a dark hallway. Will the girls figure out who it is?

"I wish I could play like that," said Noelle.

"You could if you practiced as much as I do," Hailey replied.

Hailey had amazed Marie and Noelle at the piano recital—and everyone else who was packed into the school's music room.

After the recital, Marie and Noelle had stayed and talked with Hope, Sage, Faith, Matt, and Nate and then, after the crowd had left, with Hailey.

"Girls, are you coming?" It was Noelle's dad, poking his head through one of the music-room doorways—the doorway that led outside to the parking lot.

"My family's waiting for me, too," said Hailey. She hugged Noelle and Marie, waved to Matt and Nate, who were speaking with the janitor, and headed out.

"We'll be right there, Dad," said Noelle, "but I have to run and get my homework. I left it in our classroom. Come with me, Marie?"

The girls raced through the other music-room doorway and out into the long hall that ran down the center of the school.

Then they stopped.

"It's dark," said Marie. "Can you even see where you're going?"

"Wait just a minute and our eyes will get used to it."

Before long the girls could see the shape of the hall. They walked slowly across the hard tiled floor.

"I don't think I like this," said Noelle. "What if someone's hiding in a doorway?"

Marie stopped walking. "Let's go back," she said.

"No, my homework's due tomorrow."

They continued to tiptoe down the hallway until their eyes grew more accustomed to the dark and they saw more shapes.

"What's that?" asked Noelle, pointing to a shadow.

"A drinking fountain."

"Oh yeah," said Noelle. "And that?"

"A . . . I don't know."

"I don't want to find out!" said Noelle. She began to run, and Marie followed.

And that's when they heard the footsteps. Behind them.

"Someone's following us!" shouted Noelle. The girls ran even faster.

Then the footsteps ran faster.

"It's probably Matt and Nate," said Noelle, "trying to scare us. But I'm not turning to look."

Noelle grabbed Marie's arm and jerked her into a side hallway. They stopped and held perfectly still.

The footsteps stopped, too.

"Do you think we lost them?" whispered Noelle.

"I don't know," said Marie. "Maybe they're just waiting for us. Look and see if they're still there."

"No, you look," said Noelle.

Marie slowly poked her head around the corner and scanned the main hall. She pulled her head back. "No one's there—no one that I can see, anyway."

"Maybe it's a ghost!"

"Ghosts' feet don't make footsteps," said Marie.

"How do you know?" Noelle asked. "Has a ghost ever followed you?" Noelle took a deep breath. "It's probably just the janitor," she reasoned.

"Whoever's been chasing us, I think they're gone," said Marie. She dragged Noelle out into the hall, and they started walking toward their classroom. Then they ran.

And there were the footsteps again!

"Stop!" whispered Marie. She grabbed Noelle.

They stopped.

The footsteps stopped.

"We have to go!" said Noelle. "They're still behind us!"

Marie smiled. "I don't think so. Now I know whose footsteps were following us!" she said.

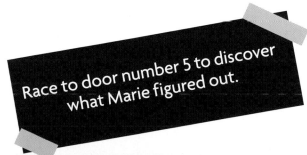

Race to door number 5 to discover what Marie figured out.

Pisa and Sew Does

**An elderly neighbor sends Marie a very odd message.
Is it an offer she can or can't refuse?**

"We're halfway to Hawaii!" Marie announced. She'd added up the money she and Noelle had earned so far.

"Halfway to Hawaii is right in the middle of the Pacific Ocean," Noelle said. "How well can you swim?"

"Not well enough to swim halfway to Hawaii," Marie joked. "We still have plenty of time to make money," she said. By December, we'll be in Hawaii with lots of cash for souvenirs."

"Souvenirs! I'm bringing back pineapples," Noelle said. "I'm climbing the tree myself."

"Pineapples grow on plants, not trees," Marie said.

"Then I'll climb a banana tree and pick bananas."

"Bananas don't grow on trees, either— giant stalks."

"Doesn't anything in Hawaii grow on trees?"

"Coconuts," said Marie.

"Then I'll climb a coconut tree. I've always wanted to climb a tree in Hawaii."

"Since when?"

"Since just now."

"I'll climb something easier," said Marie, "like a mountain."

"Before you girls exhaust yourselves climbing," Marie's mother said behind them, "hike over to my computer. Mrs. Olson, from up the street, sent you an e-mail . . . I think."

"You think?" Marie asked.

"You have to see it," Mrs. Cantu said.

The girls followed Mrs. Cantu into her office. She showed them the e-mail, which was addressed to the girls.

After they read the message, Marie and Noelle were silent. Then they said "Huh?" in unison.

"How would we know how Pisa is?" asked Marie. "And I don't know anything about sew does."

"An all-feature lunch sounds good, but what's a long more?" Marie asked. "And what does she mean by 'carry work loves'? Does she want us to carry our work? She didn't even say what the work was or how much it would weigh."

"Are we sure it's from Mrs. Olson?" asked Noelle.

"Mrs. Olson's arthritis is so bad, she can't type on a computer," said Marie.

"Just a minute," said Mrs. Cantu. "Mrs. Olson mentioned the other day that her son had a tool to help her use a computer. She speaks into the whatchamacallit, and it writes what she says or what it thinks she says."

"That's it!" Marie said. "Now it makes perfect sense!"

What was Mrs. Olson trying to say?
The answer is behind door number 11.

Give Me a Ring

Marie and Noelle find treasure up in a tree.
But is it really finders, keepers?

"So, are we going roller-skating or not?" asked Noelle. "It's getting late."

The girls had just walked home from school and now stood outside Marie's house.

"Sure," said Marie. "I don't have any homework tonight. And it looks like the weather will be—" Marie looked up to the sky. "What's that?"

"What?" asked Noelle.

Marie pointed toward the top of the tree next to the road in front of Noelle's house. "That purple thing there, hanging from that top tree limb."

Noelle looked. "Probably just something one of my brothers tossed up there."

Marie squinted. "There's a string tied to it, and something's tied to the end of the string. Something gold."

"Gold?" said Noelle. "Maybe our tree's sprouting gold nuggets. Or a squirrel tried to hide a golden acorn. We can sell it and use the money for our trip to Hawaii!" She squinted. "I'm going to climb up and see what it is."

Noelle sprinted to the tree, grabbed a low branch, and pulled

herself up onto it.

"Be careful," said Marie.

"I've been climbing this tree since I was three," said Noelle. "And I haven't fallen yet."

"Yeah, but it was shorter then."

Noelle climbed, branch to branch, up the tree, until she reached the branch with the purple thing hanging on it. She lay down on the branch and inched her way out.

"It's a popped balloon!" Noelle shouted down to Marie. She pulled up the string. "And the gold thing is a ring! With diamonds on it!"

"So *you* found my ring!" said a voice behind Marie.

Marie turned. A girl a couple of years older stood there, hand above her eyes, squinting into the tree.

"How do we know it's your ring?" asked Marie.

"Well," said the girl, "how many rings tied to balloons

do you think there are around here?"

By now Noelle had climbed down with the balloon and the ring.

"She says the ring's hers," said Marie.

"How did it get into the tree?" asked Noelle.

"I blew up a balloon for my baby brother to play with," said the girl. "I didn't want it to float away, so I tied my ring to it to keep it on the ground. But the ring wasn't heavy enough, so the balloon floated away. I've been watching it soar around the block. I lost it for a little while, but then you found it for me. Now, if you'll just give it to me, I need to get home."

"I don't think so," said Marie. "That ring might fly, but your story sure doesn't."

What was wrong with the girl's story?
Open door number 15 for the truth.

Incredible Ice Cream

A hot day zaps the girls' motivation to work—until Mrs. Ferris finds a frosty solution.

"Is it just me, or does it feel like we're melting?" Noelle asked from behind a pile of sweet corn at the farmers' market.

Hailey's mom had hired the girls to sell vegetables from the Ferrises' garden and gifts from the family's import business.

"Next time I'll bring a canopy," said Mrs. Ferris. "I didn't expect it to be so hot today."

Noelle took a long swallow from her water bottle, finishing it off. "I'm going to fill up my bottle again. Anyone?"

"Everyone should refill," said Mrs. Ferris. "We don't want anyone to overheat."

Noelle collected all the bottles and headed to find a faucet.

On her return, the girls watched Noelle wind her way around people and stalls, struggling to move through the crowd without dropping any of the bottles.

"Thanks for the help, guys," a dripping-wet Noelle said.

The girls laughed as each one grabbed her bottle.

"It looks as if yours is on your head," Marie said.

"I stuck my head under a faucet to cool off," Noelle said. "The only thing I need now is ice cream from the snack bar."

"How much?" Marie asked, reaching into her pocket.

"Three dollars for an ice cream sandwich."

"Three dollars!" Marie, Hailey, and Hope said in unison.

"They have a captive audience today," grumbled Noelle.

"I'm tempted," Marie said. "But it would take a huge chunk out of what we're earning today."

"Tough decision," said Noelle. "Buy overpriced ice cream here, or wait and buy overpriced ice cream in Hawaii."

All the ice cream talk made the girls hungry. They lifted the cooler onto the table and dug through it for their lunches.

After eating, the girls were still hot. They moved slowly as they picked up their garbage and went back to their workstations.

"You girls need more water," said Mrs. Ferris. "I'll go this time."

The girls handed her their bottles, and she headed off.

Several minutes later Mrs. Ferris returned. She passed out the water, and then she placed a plastic bag on the table.

"Ice cream sandwiches!" the girls shouted.

"You needn't do this," said Hope. "It'll eat up the profits."

"Don't worry," Mrs. Ferris said. "I picked them up at the store this morning and kept them in the back of our air-conditioned van. I just remembered when I went for water."

"This tastes so good!" said Noelle. "It's soooo cold! I really needed it."

"You're good workers and deserve it," Mrs. Ferris said.

After the girls ate their ice cream, they felt energized. They helped customers and rearranged vegetables.

"Thanks for the treat," Marie whispered to Mrs. Ferris. "I know you bought the ice cream here at the market."

Mrs. Ferris smiled. "Nothing slips by you, does it?"

For the cold, hard truth, look behind door number 14.

A Yawn on the Lawn

Marie's friends catch her napping on the job.
Will it cost Marie, or will she have the last word?

"I should've gone to bed earlier last night," Noelle said. "I can't keep my eyes open."

"Hey, you're the one who insisted we play best three out of five in that computer game," Marie said, stifling a yawn.

"Let's just ban computer games," Brooke said. "They're addictive."

The girls leaned against the car windows and dozed as they rode to their Wednesday-morning job.

Mrs. Allen had hired them to do yard work once a week during the summer.

After they arrived at the house, the girls stumbled from the car, pulled out the hand tools, and mumbled "thanks" and "bye" to Mrs. Cantu.

"I'll mow in the back," Noelle said. "The noise will keep me awake." She walked into the garage to get the lawn mower.

"I'll grab Mrs. Allen's leaf blower and remove the birdseed that fell onto her patio from the feeder," Brooke said. "That should keep everyone awake."

"And if you two plan to run those noisy machines in the

back, I'll weed the front garden," Marie said. She hated loud noises—even from the other side of the house.

Marie slipped on her gardening gloves and knelt in the cool grass. She leaned into the garden and weeded, then yawned and weeded for about twenty minutes more. Finally, she removed her gloves and sat still for a moment, resting. She surveyed the yard, recalling all the hours they'd spent cleaning the yard the first week—it had needed much work after a long winter. But now the yard needed only minor upkeep: weeding, mowing, and patio cleaning.

Marie yawned again and thought, *Just for a minute.* She crawled under a tree and stared up at the deep blue sky through the branches. She soaked in the silence. The warmth. The gentle breeze. The blues.

81

The greens. The peace. And then, Marie was asleep.

"Sleeping Beauty! Oh, Sleeping Beauty! You won't find any princes around, so you need to wake up on your own." Marie felt someone nudge her side. She opened her eyes and saw Noelle and Brooke standing above her.

"Hey, Princess! Do you hear me? I've worked hard all morning and you've been napping!" Brooke said.

"Really!" added Noelle. "And I've pushed that mower nonstop. I begged for it to break down so that I could stop, but it kept rumbling on. And here you lay, asleep!"

"Let's dock her pay," Brooke joked to Noelle. "Does a quarter an hour sound fair to you?"

"Perfectly."

Marie sat up and yawned again. "Great nap. Worth every penny. But I won't be the only paying customer. I *know* you both didn't work the entire time, either."

How did Marie know that she wasn't the only one who had taken a break? Open door number 8 to find out.

Witch Lady

**Everyone expects to see witches on Halloween.
But what happens if you think you see a real one?**

It was Halloween, and it was just starting to get dark. Hope, Marie, and Noelle were taking Hope's little brother, Davy, up and down the neighborhood streets, trick-or-treating. The girls, of course, were too old to be scared by Halloween horrors, but they had fun seeing Davy's delighted reaction to the ghosts, ghouls, and monsters.

And then they turned the corner and saw the mansion.

"Who lives here?" asked Hope.

Odd. They had no idea who lived here. And they'd visited this neighboring street many times.

"Trick-or-treat?" said Davy, pointing toward the house.

Maybe they hadn't noticed the old mansion because of the tall wrought-iron gate. It did send "Keep Out" vibes.

Or maybe the dark, overgrown ivy had hidden the house from easy view.

Or maybe they always had been too busy chatting and simply had never noticed the place before.

But now they noticed—the turrets, the black shutters, the wild garden, the scarecrow, the menacing jack-o'-lanterns, and the things hiding in the shadows.

Suddenly, a swishing shadow walked toward them. "It's Wanda's house!" the shadow shouted.

The startled girls peered down. A miniature pirate had appeared from nowhere. He wore a patch over his eye and held a paper box shaped like a treasure chest.

"Wanda? Who's Wanda?" Marie asked the boy.

"Wanda. You know, Wanda," said the pirate. "She's the witch lady."

A shiver ran up the girls' spines.

"A . . . a . . . a witch lady?" asked Hope. "And you like her?"

"Yeah," said the boy. "She's nice and intewesting."

"Is she scary?" asked Marie.

"No," said the boy. "And she has a kitty."

"A black kitty?" asked Noelle, mentally taking notes.

"How did you know?" said the boy. "The kitty's name is Wail. He's a skinny cat."

"I like kitties, too," said Davy. He tugged on his sister's hand, trying to pull her toward the house, but she didn't budge.

The girls peered into the yard. Was that a flash of black they saw in the shadows?

"And she has a puppy named Wussell," said the boy.

"I like puppies, too," said Davy. He tugged harder on Noelle's hand.

"Wussell?" said Hope. "What kind of dog name is that?"

Noelle said, "This is getting weirder and weirder."

"You should go see Wanda," said the boy. "She gave me a big bag of candy."

"Bag of candy! Bag of candy!" said Davy. This time the boy tried to let go of Noelle, but just as he thought he could make his escape, his sister grabbed him by his dragon tail.

"She's just trying to fatten you up," said Hope.

"I think we should trick-or-treat her," said Marie.

"Are you crazy?" said Noelle. "I don't want to trick-or-treat a witch. She'll probably turn me into a frog."

"Yeah," added Hope, "or a bat."

"I like bats," said Davy.

"Oh, I don't think you need to worry," said Marie. She slipped Davy's hand into hers, pushed open the gate, and headed toward the house.

Why wasn't Marie worried about the "witch lady"?
The tricky truth is behind door number 9.

Cinderelephant

An actress is late for a play. Was it really an accident or accidentally on purpose?

"Where's Sage?" asked Hope. "The play starts in just five minutes."

"I saw her this afternoon," said Noelle. "She said she'd be here."

To combat post-holiday winter doldrums, the kids had convinced their school to let them put on a play. Noelle and Brooke had written the play, *Cinderelephant.* Hope was the director, and most of their friends were in it.

"Sage doesn't have to go onstage until the second act," said Noelle. "Maybe she'll show up by then."

"I hope so," said Hope, who was a little nervous. She'd been in many plays before, but this was the first time she'd directed one. "If not, what will I do?"

"Her role's not that important," said Brooke, adjusting her large head as she walked up. "So even if she doesn't make it, we'll be just fine."

And then, it was showtime.

The curtain rose on Noelle, or Cinderelephant, scrubbing her floor at the zoo.

Enter the wicked step-rhinos—Rose and Brooke. The audience laughed at the girls' silly costumes.

The first half of the play was filled with songs, dances, and elephant jokes.

Then it was intermission.

"Sage still isn't here!" said Hope. "What are we going to do? The ballroom scene's coming up next!"

"Go on without her," said Noelle.

"But Russell will look silly dancing by himself!"

"If all you need is a dancer, I can help," said Hailey. She went out into the audience, grabbed her sister Caitlin, and led her backstage. "Here, put Caitlin in Sage's costume."

"Cool!" shouted Caitlin. "I get to star in a middle-school play. Wait till I tell my friends."

"I wouldn't exactly say 'star,'" said Hailey.

But in a couple of minutes, Caitlin was ready, looking appropriately hilarious in her hippo costume. Hailey and Russell showed her what to do, and the second half of the play began.

Caitlin did a wonderful job. No one knew that she was a last-minute substitution.

After the play ended, the audience clapped and cheered. The performers, writers, and director all took their bows. And the curtain closed.

"Sorry I'm late," said Sage, suddenly rushing onto the stage. "Is it over? I'm so sorry! I ran all the way here. My parents were late getting back from shopping, and I couldn't leave Joey alone." Joey was her little brother.

"It's OK," said Hope. "Caitlin filled in for you."

"Sorry again," said Sage. "At least I can help clean up."

In no time, everything was in order, and the girls all headed home together. A full moon shining on the snow-covered ground lit their path. Marie and Sage led the way.

"Look," said Sage. "I'm walking back home in the same footprints I made coming here."

Marie watched Sage's short, close steps as Sage carefully placed each foot in the footprint she had made on the way to the school.

Sage continued walking in her footprints until the group reached her house. "Next time we do a play, I'll ask my parents not to be late."

The girls said good night and then continued on their way—all except for Marie. "You guys go on," she said. "I need to ask Sage something."

After their friends left, Marie turned to Sage. "Why didn't you want to be in the play?"

"What do you mean, Marie? I did all I could to get to the school on time. It wasn't my fault that I had to babysit."

"Oh, I think you had plenty of time to make it," said Marie. "And you can tell me the truth, you know."

"A minor role, a silly-looking costume, and I had to dance with Russell," Sage blurted out. "I feel awful, but I didn't want to hurt Hope's feelings. Anyway, how did you know?"

Find out how Marie knew by looking behind door number 12.

The Gentle Pony

Marie's friends convince her to ride a pony.
Will her puzzle skills land her in the safest saddle?

"You rode ponies?" Marie asked.

The girls were working at the Ferrises' stall at the farmers' market. They were telling Marie about their trip to the stables. Marie hadn't gone because she'd been sick. "We loved it!" Hope said. "You should see these sweet animals, Marie. I wish my parents would buy me one."

"Where would you keep it?" Noelle asked. "The patio?"

"It's so sad you were sick," Hailey said to Marie loudly enough for her mom to hear. "We should take you riding today."

"When things slow down," Mrs. Ferris said. "But let's set up. I see customers arriving already."

"Yes, we're way too busy," Marie said quickly. She organized the produce, moved over to work on the imported odds and ends, and then jumped over to the homemade crafts. "Don't just watch me. We have tons more to do!"

As the girls worked, the pony discussion continued.

"Ride a pony," Hope said to Marie. "You can choose among four different ones, but ride mine. She's beautiful—black and white. I love black-and-white horses. Both Polka Man and Cookies and Cream are black and white."

"I'm not, um . . . *comfortable* with horses," Marie admitted.

"You're imagining large horses," said Noelle. "Ride a gentle pony and you'll be comfortable with it."

"I'll never be comfortable. Less than terrified, maybe."

"Oh, these ponies won't scare you," added Hope.

"No, thanks," said Marie.

"Face your fears," urged Noelle. "That's what *you* always say."

"You won't leave me alone until I do," said Marie. She knew Noelle was right. "Which pony is the gentlest?"

"That would be the one that four-year-old rode," Noelle said. "She didn't want to ride, but the lady said that pony was a softy. *I* wouldn't ride it. It didn't *do* anything."

"That's the one I want to ride," Marie said. "The one that doesn't *do* anything. Which one was that?"

"Don't ride mine," Hailey said. "The one they call Gray Bones nearly bucked me off just because I scratched her behind her ears! I want to try Chocolate next."

"The brown one?" Hope asked.

"The brown one," Hailey answered.

"Which pony did the little girl ride?" Marie asked again.

"Just thinking about my pony's name makes me hungry," said Noelle.

"Excuse me," Marie said. "Which is the gentle pony?"

"Mine made me hungry, too," Hope said. "When does the snack bar open?"

"Never mind," Marie said to her friends. "I've figured out which one the girl rode, but thanks for your help."

Which pony is the gentle pony? And how did Marie figure it out?
Trot to door number 8 for the answer.

Same Time, Same Place

If you do something and don't break a rule,
how can you do exactly the same thing and break it?

"We'll have to do this again," said Hailey as she slipped on her shoes.

"It was fun," said Marie.

Noelle nodded. "Only my house next time."

It hadn't been anything major, nothing particularly outstanding. It had just been a fun afternoon with friends—homemade pizza,

charades, playing against the TV contestants on the girls' favorite show, *Guess Which Dog*, which came on every Saturday at 6:30 p.m. But just as the final credits rolled, and the sun began to set into the late summer horizon, it was time for Hailey to hurry home. Family rule: home by sunset.

Hailey said good-bye, grabbed another slice of pizza,

and raced out the door.

Then, a week before Halloween, Noelle decided it was time for another pizza party. "Remember our little party in August?" she asked Marie and Hailey.

"Party?" said Hailey.

"You remember—pizza, charades, *Guess Which Dog,* me, you, Marie?"

Hailey smiled. "Oh, yeah! That was so fun."

"How about this Saturday?" asked Noelle.

"I'm spending Friday night with my grandma," said Marie.

"Oh," said a disappointed Noelle and Hailey together.

"But I'll be home by 3:00 on Saturday. We started at 4:00 before, so if we start at the same time, I can make it."

"Great!" said Noelle. "Be at my house at 4:00."

Hailey and Marie showed up at Noelle's doorstep at 4:00 on the dot. Marie was about to knock when Noelle opened the door and welcomed them in.

The girls tried to repeat their exact steps from the last party— after all, it had been so perfectly timed that the pizzas were ready just as their show began. First, they started the pizza. They mixed the pizza dough ingredients—yeast, sugar, flour, salt, oil, and water.

Next, they played charades while the pizza dough rose.

Then, as soon as the dough had risen, they divided it into three blobs so that each could create her favorite pizza: cheese and mushroom for Hailey, ham and pineapple for Noelle, pepperoni for Marie. They cleaned up while the pizzas baked. Finally, just as the theme song to their show began, the pizzas were ready.

The girls ate as they watched *Guess Which Dog.*

When the final credits rolled, Hailey got up and pulled on her boots. "My house next time!" she said.

"Sure," said Marie. "Oh, no! I'm sorry, Hailey. I should have known this would happen." Marie hit her forehead with her palm and grabbed her jacket. "Noelle, you and I had better walk Hailey home. Then maybe she won't get into trouble."

Why did Marie think Hailey would be in trouble? Take your time before opening door number 3.

It Walks at Midnight

Bigfoot roams the park. Or is it Stiff Foot?

Noelle's brother Patrick woke up Noelle to tell her the news. When he'd gone out early that winter morning on a walk through the park, he'd seen it—Bigfoot, Sasquatch, whatever it was. At least he'd seen its giant footprints.

"I followed them for a ways," Patrick said, "but I stopped because I didn't *really* want to meet it."

Noelle was thrilled. Part of her wanted to find the famous monster, get to know it, become friends with it, and understand what made it hide from people.

The smarter part of her wanted to stay far, far away, because who knew what a monster like that would do to you if it caught you?

The first part of her won.

She dressed quickly and ran next door to Marie's house. Marie was still asleep, so Noelle woke her up.

"Patrick's made a great discovery! Come on, Marie—we've gotta check this out. We're smart. We'll look at the clues and figure out how to find it."

"I don't think I want to find a giant," said Marie. "I like my arms attached to my body."

"Who has it ever hurt?" asked Noelle. "Please, for me? It's probably just a kind, shy, bunny-rabbit type who only wants a friend."

"I very much doubt that," said Marie. "But I'll go with you to the park, at least."

Marie dressed, and then the two girls raced out of the house and off to the park.

Apparently the news hadn't gotten around yet. No one else was there. The girls quickly found the set of huge footprints.

They were indeed large—about twenty inches long and ten inches wide. Each print had a big toe on the right side of the foot, with three more little toes. Only four toes! The footprints flattened the snow smooth.

In the middle were smaller footprints, probably Patrick's, from when he'd tracked the beast.

The girls followed the huge footprints across the park. Was it the cold of the morning or the thought of meeting a monster that sent shivers up Noelle's spine?

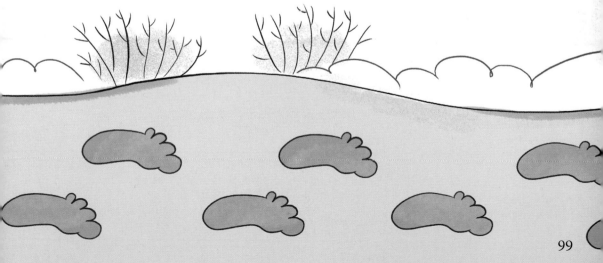

"CAW-CAW-CAW."

"What's that?" shouted Noelle. She grabbed on to Marie's coat.

"It's just a crow," whispered Marie.

They followed more prints past picnic tables, around a pavilion, between silent trees. And then, CRACK!

Noelle jumped.

A tree branch, heavy with snow, fell behind them.

The girls continued to follow the prints. Once they reached the main road, the prints disappeared on the cleanly plowed pavement.

Noelle looked around to see if the footprints resumed across the street, but she couldn't find any more.

"It's got to be behind us! Let's backtrack," said Noelle. "Maybe we can find where the tracks started from."

Suddenly, an eerie sound came from behind them. "Arrrooooo!" Marie couldn't decide if it was a howl or a moan.

"Never mind," Noelle said as she grabbed Marie's arm. "Let's get out of here!"

Marie smiled. "Fine with me," she said, "but I already know what's out there and where these prints came from."

What made the sound, where did the monster's footprints come from, and how did Marie know this?
All the answers are behind door number 7.

Lost in the Library

Why would someone hide Lincoln Middle School's most popular book—in the library?

"*Harriet Putter*! It's in! Oh, I want it next!" Marie clutched the book and looked at Mrs. Morris, the school librarian. *Harriet Putter*, the story of a girl with magical powers, was the hottest thing at Lincoln Middle School.

Brooke grabbed for it. "No, Marie, that book has my name written all over it. I get it next."

"Your name? It has my name and I get it."

"We'll see who gets it," said Brooke. "Mrs. Morris, since I'm your favorite library aide and since I'm working in the library now and Marie's just hanging out, I get *Harriet Putter*, don't I?"

"I'd love to let both of you have it, but you know the rules," sighed Mrs. Morris. "It goes to the next person on the waiting list. Have you two signed up?"

"Days ago," Marie said. "And I'm still twelfth on the list."

"I'm eleventh on the list," Brooke said. "Ha! I get it first."

"After ten other people," Marie said.

"Maybe, maybe not."

"I've ordered more copies, girls," Mrs. Morris said. "When they come in, you'll move up the list more quickly. In the meantime, leave the book with me and get to class. The bell's about to ring. Brooke, back to work. Marie, I'll see you at two."

Marie was scheduled to work that afternoon as a library aide.

At two o'clock sharp Marie was back in the library for her class hour as an aide. "Shelve these books for me, would you?" asked Mrs. Morris. "They all go in the science section."

Marie pushed the book cart over to the corner where the science books were located and began to put books on the shelves where they belonged: a book about space, one about nuclear energy, one about lizards . . . what was this? *Harriet Putter*? In the science section? She pulled it off the shelf and took it up to Mrs. Morris.

"It was between *Lizards of Albania* and *Lizards of the Arctic*," said Marie. "How do you think it got there?"

"It didn't get there by magic," said Mrs. Morris. "I'll ask at our library aides meeting tomorrow."

"I thought you had a conference and were going to have a substitute."

"That was the plan, but they cancelled the conference, so here I'll be. See you tomorrow morning."

In the morning Mrs. Morris told the aides to have a seat. There were seven aides: three boys—Matt, Nate, and Russell—and four girls—Marie, Faith, Brooke, and Hope.

"Yesterday, somehow, *Harriet Putter* was moved from my desk, where I had it saved for Allie Bentley, who was next on the list to check it out," said Mrs. Morris. "It ended up on the shelves. Does anyone have any idea how it got there?"

"I wasn't at school yesterday," explained Russell.

"It wasn't my day to help," said Hope.

"I was here yesterday," said Brooke. "I shelved the whole time in the fiction section, but I left the book on your desk. Didn't touch it. Promise."

"I was here, too," said Matt. "But I was shelving in the history section, not the science section. I couldn't have put it there."

"I came in yesterday to check out a book," said Nate, "but my day to shelve is tomorrow."

"And today's my day," said Faith.

"Well, keep an eye out, and be careful when you're shelving," said Mrs. Morris. "We don't want this accident repeated, however it happened. And we don't want to lose a book as popular as *Harriet Putter.*"

It wasn't an accident, Marie thought to herself. She didn't tell this to Mrs. Morris, though. She just glanced over and smiled at the person in the group she knew had put the book on the shelf.

Who does Marie think put *Harriet Putter* on the science shelves?
The answer is behind door number 1.

Chalk One Up

An after-school job leaves two girls covered
in chalk dust. What really happened?

"Did I wear a jacket this morning?" Noelle asked Marie on their
way home from school.

"Yeah," said Marie. "So did I."

"Well, how many of us are wearing jackets right now?"

Marie counted. "One, two . . . zero."

Together Marie and Noelle said, "We left them at school!"

The girls turned and headed back to their homeroom.

As they walked in, two ghosts suddenly appeared in front
of them.

"What in the . . ." muttered Marie.

"Faith, Sage, what's going on?" Noelle asked.

Faith and Sage dropped the chalk erasers they were pounding
each other with and turned toward the girls. They had guilty looks on
their faces. Sage's normally blonde hair was pink, and Faith's black
hair was gray.

"That's what I want to know, too," said a voice behind Marie
and Noelle. It was Ms. Toone. She didn't wear her usually happy
expression.

Ms. Toone walked to the front of the room, followed by Marie
and Noelle. Every inch of Ms. Toone's desk, her chair, the map of the

United States—and everything else within a four-foot radius—was covered in chalk dust. Even the phone had a smooth, thick layer of chalk dust on it.

"Before two girls get into very serious trouble, they'd better explain what happened," said Ms. Toone.

"It was the chalk vac," said Sage. The "chalk vac" is what Ms. Toone called the mini vacuum cleaner that she let the kids on chalkboard duty use to clean the dust from the chalk tray. "It fell apart and the dust blew all over the place."

"Where is it?" asked Ms. Toone.

Faith reached under Ms. Toone's desk and pulled out the little vacuum. "We put it back together."

Marie and Noelle had been on chalkboard duty two days ago, and they'd noticed then that the chalk vac would need emptying soon. They could see through the clear plastic of the vacuum that, indeed, it had been emptied—but not into the trash.

"How long ago did this happen?" asked Ms. Toone.

"About ten minutes ago," answered Sage.

"Why didn't you call the office and report it?"

"We did!" said Sage. "But, uh, there wasn't an answer. Then we called again, but it was busy."

"Well, let's try again," said Ms. Toone as she picked up the dusty phone.

While Ms. Toone made the call, Noelle turned to Sage. "If you two were so concerned about this mess, why were you having an eraser fight?"

"Once the mess was made, we couldn't resist," Faith said. She shook her hair and a faint wisp of chalk dust floated over to Marie and Noelle.

Noelle sneezed. "Stop that," she said.

"The custodian will be right here," Ms. Toone told the girls. "While we're waiting, let's start cleaning."

Ms. Toone pulled a broom from the closet. Sage checked the chalk vac to make sure it wouldn't fall apart and then started vacuuming.

When the custodian came into the room, he stopped dead in his tracks. He wasn't happy. "What happened here?" he asked.

Sage quickly explained. "We're sorry," said Sage. "It was an accident. And after it happened, we tried right away to get it taken care of. We called the office but couldn't get an answer."

"Well, I don't have time right now to clean it up. I'm in the middle of a couple of other urgent jobs. But you two girls," he pointed to dust-covered Sage and Faith, "can just stay here and clean until I get back. If I think you've done enough, I'll finish up. If not, we'll call your parents and explain to them why you'll be home late."

After the custodian left, Ms. Toone said, "I'm going to the office for some rags. We're going to need them."

Right after Ms. Toone left, Marie looked at the two ghosts. "Sage, this might have started as an accident, but you did not try to take care of it right away. Noelle and I will help you clean up. But you shouldn't have lied to Ms. Toone."

How did Marie know that Sage had been lying? Discover the truth behind door number 9.

What's for Dinner?

Four meals mean trouble for two babysitters.
Will the sitters make the correct dinner decision?

"Ethan and Ellen shouldn't be any trouble," said Mrs. Lloyd on the phone to Marie. "Excuse me a second—"

"—Brent," Mrs. Lloyd said, muffling the phone with her hand, "please take out the recycling. It's overflowing. Thank you! Thank you! Thank you!—now, where was I?" Mrs. Lloyd asked, returning to Marie.

"You said the twins won't be any trouble," Marie said.

"Oh, yeah. Put them to bed at eight and read a couple of stories, and they'll go right to sleep. We'll leave out their favorite toys and DVDs. I can't believe I'm going to see a movie tonight when I have company coming tomorrow for lunch. At least I've prepared all the food already."

"Everything will be fine, Mrs. Lloyd."

"I'll cook something for tonight's dinner as soon as I hang up the phone. I'll leave it in the fridge. Just heat it in the microwave. Noelle's coming with you, right?"

"I haven't asked. I believe she's free, if you don't mind."

"No problem. When caring for twins, four hands are better than two," Mrs. Lloyd said. "See you at five!"

At a quarter to five, Marie and Noelle arrived at the Lloyd house. The girls waited while Mrs. Lloyd rushed around. "I made your dinner, but I didn't have time to finish cleaning up the kitchen until just now," she told Marie as she tossed an empty tomato-sauce jar into the recycling bin. "I'll stick our cell-phone number on the fridge in case of emergency, and I'll keep my cell phone on vibrate," she said. "Call if you need anything."

The Lloyds kissed their five-year-olds good-bye and left.

The girls adored the twins. Ellen told silly jokes. Ethan made funny noises. And both of them laughed a lot.

At six o'clock Noelle said, "Is it time for dinner?"

"My stomach says 'yes,'" said Marie. "What do you think, kids?"

"My stomach says 'yes, yes, yes!'" said Ethan, and he ran to the kitchen and threw open the refrigerator door.

Four serving dishes sat on the top shelf. Marie looked into each dish. Roast beef filled one, baked ham another, spaghetti and meat-balls a third, and fried chicken the fourth.

"Are they all for us?" Noelle asked. "I'm starving!"

"Mrs. Lloyd said she'd cook us *a* dinner—not four dinners," said Marie. "She has company coming tomorrow."

"So which is ours?" Noelle asked. "I know, the warm one. If she just cooked it, it'll still be warm."

"Smart thinking, Noelle!" Marie touched each dish. "Oh, they're all cold. Ethan? Ellen? Do you know what your mom wanted us to have for dinner?"

"Maybe ice cream!" Ethan shouted.

"I don't think so," said Marie.

"Should we call Mrs. Lloyd?" Noelle asked. "She said we should if we needed anything. We need to know what to eat!"

Marie thought of something else Mrs. Lloyd had said before she'd left. Then Marie shook her head. "We don't need to bother her," she said, pulling a serving dish out of the refrigerator. "I know what Mrs. Lloyd wanted us to have for dinner." Fifteen minutes later, Marie served a reheated home-cooked meal to Ellen, Ethan, and Noelle.

What was for dinner—and how did Marie figure it out? Open door number 17 for the answer.

Love Letter

**Did the shyest girl in class write a love letter
to one of her classmates?**

Rebecca Sorensen was smart. She could name all fifty states
in twenty seconds—thirty seconds if she added the capitals. She'd
been district spelling-bee champion two years in a row. And it wasn't
uncommon for Rebecca to correct Ms. Toone when the teacher made
a mistake during math.

But when Rebecca wasn't answering questions, she was quiet.
Rebecca was the shyest kid in class.

So when Brooke found, blown against a bush on the playground,
the love letter from Rebecca to Matt, everyone was surprised.

"Well, I'd never believe it if I didn't see it myself," said Hope. "Shy
Rebecca has a boyfriend!"

"At least she has good taste," said Sage.

"Speak for yourself," Faith said. "Matt burps louder than anyone
I've ever heard. It's disgusting."

Hailey grabbed the note and read it out loud. "How sweet!" she
said when she was finished. Hailey held the note to her chest and
fluttered her eyelashes.

"Do you think Matt likes her back?" Hope asked.

"Don't see why he wouldn't." It was Noelle's turn to get her two
cents in. "Rebecca is smart, and she has a nice smile when she's not
hiding it."

"Can I see that note?" Marie asked, and she took it from Hailey.

"I can't wait to tell everyone in class. Rebecca likes Matt," Brooke began to sing.

"I don't know if we should be spreading this all over," said Noelle. "I don't think Rebecca wanted anyone to read this note."

"There's an even better reason we shouldn't be spreading this around class," said Marie. "This might be a real note from Rebecca to Matt, but it's not from *our* Rebecca."

Dear Matt
I hope your not embarased to receive this letter, but I like you very much. your a very nice person and I'm so glad we got to be partners for our science expirement. Now I hope we can be friends.

Love,
Rebecca

If you'd love to find out what Marie
knows, go to door number 10.

Cousin Sam

Jealousy, vanity, frustration—how can a cousin's visit
cause such an uproar?

"My cousin Sam is going to be here for Thanksgiving," Rose told
Marie and Noelle when she ran into them on the school playground.

"Sam the Star?" asked Noelle excitedly. "Cool!"

"I don't know if Sam's a star," said Rose. "It was only a walk-on role
in a made-for-TV movie."

"Yeah, but still, millions of people saw that movie," said Noelle.
"Sam will be famous someday."

"I think so," said Rose, "but I am biased. Anyway, we want to have a
party the day after Thanksgiving, with maybe you two, me, and some
boys from class. We'll eat leftovers, play some games, and talk."

"I'm in," said Noelle.

"I'll be there," said Marie.

"Where will you be?" asked Hope, who had walked up.

"Party at Rose's house," said Noelle, "for Rose's cousin Sam. It'll be
on Friday, the day after Thanksgiving."

"I'm there," said Hope. "I bunked with Sam at French camp two
years ago."

"Maybe we can audition for movie roles," joked Noelle.

Rose laughed. "You wish. Maybe a romantic comedy starring you and Ben."

"Somebody talking about me?" It was Ben, accompanied by Matt and Nate.

"Yeah," said Noelle. "Rose's cousin Sam is going to make us movie stars. We're all invited to Rose's house for a party and auditions."

"Hey, there'll be enough ham at the party without you guys acting out, too," said Rose. "This is strictly for fun."

"What's for fun?" asked Nate.

"Rose's party," said Ben. "My brother wants to be an actor. He should come to the party, too."

"What party?" asked Matt.

"Listen closely," said Rose. "I'm going to say this once. My cousin Sam—"

"—the movie star," said Noelle.

"—the made-for-TV-movie walk-on," Rose continued, "is going to be in town for Thanksgiving. We're throwing a party on Friday. You're invited. We'll play—"

"—charades, so that Sam can see how fine an actor I am," Noelle interrupted again.

"Right," grumbled Ben. Suddenly he wasn't so sure if he wanted to go to this party. "We get it. You love Sam."

"We'll play nonacting games to drive Noelle nuts," said Rose.

Hope piped up. "Sage and I will reenact our heart-wrenching roles as the stars of our school play, *The Pet Shop*. Let's invite the whole cast. We can do the play again. Sam will love it!"

"Anyway," said Rose, "Sam had a lot of fun last summer and wants to hang out with all you guys."

"Who's Sam?" asked Matt.

"Sam! My cousin!" said Rose, sighing with frustration. "Maybe Sam and I will just go to a movie instead."

"Sam's OK," Ben said to Matt, "but he's not that amazing. I should know. I spent a lot of time with him last summer."

"No, you *don't* know," said Marie.

What did Marie mean?
To get in on the act,
open door number 6.

Cream-Puff Day

Brooke planned to double her desserts but ended up with an empty plate. Where did things go wrong?

"Trade you . . . my peas for your dessert," Marie said to Noelle.

"I'll trade you . . . my peas and my milk for your dessert," Noelle responded.

"I'll trade you . . . our house, our car, and the six million dollars I'm going to make when I'm rich and famous for your dessert," Marie said.

"I'll trade you all that and an old shoe for your dessert," said Noelle.

It was a game they played on Cream-Puff Day. Marie and Noelle didn't know how the lunch ladies, whose food was usually OK but not special, made their cream puffs so incredible. The girls figured it must just be magic.

And they knew that there was no way either one of them would trade anything for her cream puff. But the chance to get two cream puffs? Tempting.

Brooke sat down across from them. "Trade you my peas for your cream puffs," she said.

Marie and Noelle laughed.

"You are getting sleepy," said Marie. "You don't want our cream puffs. In fact, you don't even want yours, do you? You are in my power. Now you will hand your cream puff over to me."

Brooke laughed, encircling her cream puff with her arms. She stopped and then smiled. "I'll make you a deal, though." She pulled a pencil from her pocket and tore her napkin in half. "I'm going to mark these two napkin pieces." As she talked, she held each napkin piece under the table where no one could see it, made a quick mark on it, and folded it. "Then I'll give one of you lucky girls the chance to pick one of the pieces. If you pick the piece with the X, you get my cream puff. If you pick the piece with the O, I get your cream puff.

Anyone game? Anyone want the chance to have two whole delicious cream puffs at the very same time? You have a fifty-fifty chance!"

Marie looked at Noelle. Noelle looked at Marie. "I'll do it," said Marie before Noelle could say anything.

Brooke held out one napkin piece in each hand. "Pick one."

Marie thought carefully.

"I think it's a trick," Noelle whispered to Marie.

Marie chose the napkin in Brooke's right hand.

She slowly opened it up, holding it so that no one could see, and said, "It's an X. You owe me your cream puff." Then she tore the napkin into little pieces and shoved it into her pocket.

"Wait!" said Brooke. "I don't believe you. You didn't show any of us your napkin."

"Oh, sorry," said Marie, and she smiled at Brooke. "But I'll tell you what we can do. You show me your napkin piece, and if it has an O on it, it'll prove mine had an X."

Brooke sighed as she opened up her napkin. On it was an O.

Then Brooke laughed. "That was clever, Marie. Here's your cream puff."

What was Brooke up to, and how did Marie get two cream puffs? The answer is behind door number 5.

120

Easy as Pie

Someone secretly ate a pumpkin pie. But in a house filled with people, how will anyone figure out who?

"Junior, get out of the kitchen," Marie said firmly as she shooed out the family's dog. Then she returned to help her mom with Thanksgiving dinner.

Mom and Marie had made the pies—one pumpkin, two apple, and one pecan—yesterday. The pies were in the pantry, where they'd stay until dessert time.

The turkey in the oven was almost ready. The rolls and yams were done, the table was set, and Marie was adding one last pat of butter to the mashed potatoes. Dinner would be ready soon.

There would be plenty of it. And there would need to be. Marie's brothers alone could eat most of it. They always seemed to be hungry, especially Chris, who was bigger than Zachary, even though he was two years younger.

And then there was everyone else around the table—Marie's parents, her grandparents, her aunt and uncle and their five kids, and Marie herself. Fifteen people could put away a lot of food. And that wasn't counting Junior, who would get his fill of Thanksgiving leftovers.

Mom pulled the turkey from the oven. It smelled soooo good. "Call everyone to the dining room, would you, Marie?" she asked.

Marie was happy to oblige. She shouted upstairs to her brothers. "Tyler, Zachary, Chris, time for dinner!" Immediately Tyler and Zachary emerged from Tyler's room and leaped down the stairs, followed by their five cousins. Marie didn't even want to know what kinds of mischief they had been creating.

Marie's father and uncle poked their heads in from the living room. "Did we hear right? Do we finally get to eat?" Dad asked. "Mmmm, that turkey smells good."

The kids and Marie's grandparents found their seats. Marie's dad, mom, uncle, and aunt were soon seated, and finally her brother Chris pulled up his chair and sat down.

Each person said what he or she was thankful for, and then the feast began.

Dad carved the turkey.

Tyler and Zachary scooped huge piles of mashed potatoes onto their plates.

The cousins soon had their plates filled, too.

Chris took a piece of turkey and some cranberry sauce.

Grandma and Grandpa waited patiently to serve themselves until their grandchildren had begun to eat.

Marie picked a piece of turkey off her plate and reached it down to Junior under the table. "There's more where that came from," she told the excited dog. "And leave room for pie." Junior loved pumpkin pie.

As soon as the moans and groans about full stomachs had begun, Mom announced, "I'm ready for dessert. Who wants pie?"

A chorus of cheers erupted.

"Marie, would you help me?"

When Marie and her mother reached the pantry, Mom looked at the pies, frowned, and asked, "Didn't we make four pies?"

"Two apple, a pumpkin, and a pecan," Marie said.

"Well now, it looks as if the pie bandits have been here. We're missing a pumpkin pie."

Mom left the pies in the pantry, and she and Marie returned to the dining room.

"We have a mystery," Mom said. "Marie and I made four pies. Now there are only three. One pie is missing. Any idea where it went?"

"I'll bet Marie ate it," said her brother Zachary. "She couldn't resist."

"Have you checked Junior's hiding spots?" Marie's brother Chris asked. "He's been in the kitchen, hasn't he? And we know how much he loves pumpkin pie."

Everyone looked down at Junior, who was so sure he had done something wrong that he slunk under the table.

Marie's uncle looked at his kids. "What were you kids all doing up in Tyler's room? I predict that a careful inspection will reveal an empty pie plate hidden under the bed."

One of the cousins spoke up. "I predict that careful inspection will reveal an empty pie plate hidden under the sofa in the living room where the grown-ups were watching football."

"I think it's pretty clear who ate the pie," Marie said.

"Clear to me, too," Mom said. She smiled. "On the count of three, if you know who ate the pie, point to the culprit. One . . . two . . . three!"

Marie and Mom both pointed to the same person.

Who took the pie, and how did Marie and her mom know?
Go to door number 4 for the truth.

What a Character!

A great job awaits the girls—if they can find the right location. Will they make it on time?

"You two owe me big-time!" Brooke told Marie and Noelle as they gathered up tools. Brooke's grandmother had a friend, Mrs. Allen, who needed yard work done. She had a big yard and promised to pay the girls well if they did a good job.

"Sure," Noelle said. "Next time Dad asks me to mow our lawn, you'll be the first one I call." She smiled and then said, "But really, thanks for asking us to help."

"Especially if we do a good job," Brooke said. "Grandma says Mrs. Allen might ask us back every week."

"Ready?" Mrs. Cantu asked from behind the wheel of the van. She had volunteered to drive the girls.

"Almost, Mom," Marie said. The girls put the last of the tools in the back and piled into the van.

"Buckle up!" Mrs. Cantu shouted, as she always did just before her van set off. "Now, give me the address."

"It's . . . oh, three-three-three-something," Brooke said.

"Well, that narrows it down for us," Mrs. Cantu said under her breath.

"Mrs. Allen said to head down Ninth Avenue," added Brooke. "Maybe I'll know the street when I see it."

"Don't you remember anything about the name?" Mrs. Cantu

asked. "What letter does it start with?"

"The name reminded me of a children's book character," Brooke said. "But I can't remember which one."

"I don't know any streets around here named after book characters," said Mrs. Cantu, sounding a bit more stressed.

"It wasn't a character. It was *almost* a character."

"Wonderful," said Mrs. Cantu sarcastically. The way she said "wonderful" made the girls burst out laughing.

"It's not smart to show up late on your first day," said Noelle. She was stressed, too. With only a short time left before summer ended, Noelle worried whether she and Marie could earn enough to afford the trip to Hawaii.

"Madeleine Street?" asked Marie. "Lois Lane?"

This put everyone in the right mood. The girls threw out names of other famous book characters.

"No," Brooke said, feeling frustrated.

"Well, here's Ninth," said Mrs. Cantu. "Start looking."

The girls shouted out the street names as they passed each sign.

Suddenly Marie shouted, "Stop!"

Mrs. Cantu slammed on the brakes. "What's wrong?"

"Turn around!" Marie exclaimed. "I know where her house is!"

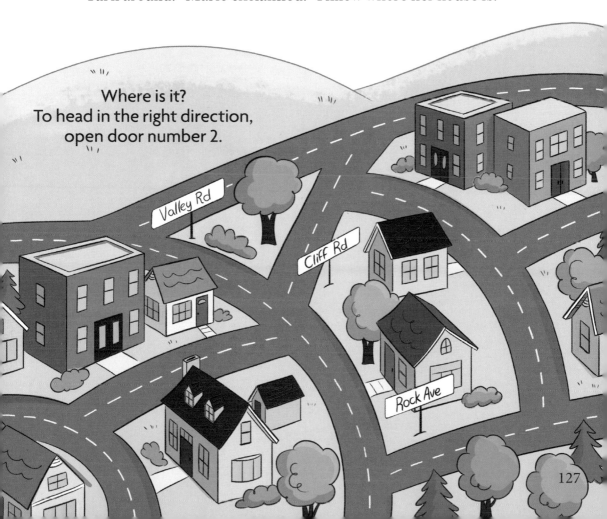

Where is it?
To head in the right direction,
open door number 2.

Here are some other American Girl books you might like: